Almost Exactly Like This

Alison Brown

Almost Exactly Like This
First published in Great Britain in 2017

Lincolnshire

Copyright © Alison Brown 2017

The right of Alison Brown to be identified as the author of this work has been asserted by her in accordance with the Copyright, Design and Patents Act of 1988
All rights reserved

Cover design and illustrations Hattie Brown

CONTENTS

Hopefully

Almost Everything

Two

Identity Theft

Hopefully

I really hope I am wrong about you.
I hope it says more about me
than it does about you
that I would even think
some of the things
I am going to write down.

Hopefully you won't recognise
the smallest vestige of yourself
in the picture I am about to paint.

You will read with a growing sense of horror,
And wonder
why anyone would have such thoughts,
let alone think them about you.
Never mind write them down
to be read and reread
and queried and quoted.

Hopefully you will turn to someone close by,
Someone who knows you as well as anyone does,
and you will ask them to read the words too.

And you will enquire bleakly,
'Does this sound *anything* like me?
Am I even *remotely* like this?
Do *you* think this is true?'

And they will shake their head
and pull a face
and scrunch up their forehead
and respond with,
'No, no, that is *nothing* like you.
How peculiar.
How could anyone see *any* of this in *you*?'

Hopefully they will not be secretly delighted
that someone has dared to express

what they would certainly have not.
That someone has taken the time
to lay it out in black and white
and doesn't care a jot
that it can be read and reread

and stands by their words
whatever the consequence.

Hopefully that will not happen.

Almost Everything

Light illuminates and overwhelms.
Colours pierce uniform correctness:
bedding plants, reds, pinks and whites.

Beyond? The wombing sound of leaves.
Beyond? The road: silver and enduring.
Traffic flowing.
Nothing stops.
Everything is exactly as it was.
Almost everything.

Four figures stand,
lonely. They have tried
to reshape their ruined faces,
but it is too soon.
They are locked into their waiting.
They are not a unit
by any means.

There seem to be two couples.

A sister with her husband

who has cried and cried and now hangs on to him,

gripping tightly with her gloved hands,

thankful she is well and beautiful and married.

Husband: grim-faced and bewildered.

Oh my, the other two.

Not a couple; simply coupled:

a mother and her son, her boy.

The husband, a crumpling.

An aching wretchedness;

what is left of everything that was:

days and weeks and years of everyday that.

He remains and is, and she has gone and is not.

He feels and he cannot speak.

He will not get used to this.

It will not get less awful or less true.

He will howl,

but not now.

He is walking and moving and he can breathe for now.

Two are absent from the scene.

One of them is you.

At six

you catch ladybirds, shout desires

and gobble food;

you run and smile, and know a lot.

You feel everything,

acutely but vaguely.

In forty years' time you will find this solemn place,

on a satellite map.

Omnipotent, you will tilt up,

up

and away from it as though suspended in the heavens

and you will fly across the country in a second or less

to pinpoint another town two hundred miles away

where you will have been sent to

escape the unexpected.

They don't know what to say, you see
so they will say nothing.

Remember the smaller one.
Separate and too little to be of interest to you yet.
She already feels the loss,
the physical loss.
Not ready to be separate self, she has already noticed

the lack of what was there,
but will soon forget how it felt
or who it was.

This moment:
the sun and the flowers and the passing cars;
the trees and the traffic.
It is always happening now.

You missed this moment?
All of those years holding on to what you missed.
Go now, forty years later, instead.

Go to this same place, or another one,
and feel the warmth of the sun
and notice the flowers
and the passers-by
and the way the cars don't stop.

Observe a husband and his mother, the sister and her gloves,
her husband and his awkwardness.
Join them as they follow the official
through into the chapel
and hear some indisputable facts about a life that was
and watch the coffin disappear.

If there is no husband, there will be a wife.
No sister?
Find the brother or perhaps the children.
Join them.
Almost everything will be exactly the same
as it was
today.

Two

You,
too young to imagine other two year olds exist,
or matter,
or don't have a silky, four-legged shadow
to touch and stroke and hold on to.

A perfect little world of certainty, followed around
by an inky, wet full stop, leathery black-nosed silky one.
Existing together, one and the same in thought and action.

You've lots to do. Lots.
The chairs need to be upturned and that takes strength.
Positioned exactly
to allow the stolen blanket to balance as a roof

without drooping down
too low.
You have to be able to sit in it,
and let the pink light buffer the sides
of the knobbly blanket

whilst you sort things out:
beds for all the children and a place to keep
the tea things.
Of course there is room for silky one too.
She lies and watches, unsurprised by your
busy actions.
She knows this must be done as well as you.

Hovering just beyond is a
thought of why you needed to build the den.
You know you had been sure, and there was
something bigger planned,
but now it's gone.

You don't mourn its passing:

it is forgotten as

soon as felt,

and you quickly return to the present.

'of course there is room for the silky one too'

Pegs.

They would help and mummy has some.

Up you get in one swift move and propel yourself

out of the room with its table and chairs

and into the high-topped, shiny kitchen;

silky one follows.

She leans against you as you look up
and start to ask for pegs.
Please.
There's a delay,
and as you explain why they're needed
your little fingers move from nose to head on
silky one.

She stands,
enjoying this other sort of love,
different from the adult-handed pats
which move from neck to back and pat
and always stop too soon.

You stop listening to the tall one
and start to think about the beauty of the silky
one's nose.
You look at your hand and at the narrowness
of the nose
as you stroke it from the tip to the head;

the stillness and the calmness and the
brownness of the fur
hold you for a moment.
Then you are back
in the kitchen and you have pegs,
pink and yellow ones mixed up, jumbled.
Click clack, click clack
in the tin.

Back to the house, the den, to make it better
and stronger
so it is ready
for whatever it needs to be ready for:
it's important.
Eventually it's finished. Done.
It's taken all morning with breaks for milk and
moments diverted to other things,
a book, a biscuit and the TV screen,
but it is brilliant.

Silky one lies just outside its edges, head on
paws, still,
believing in your vision,
deep brown eyes darting about your face
as you put the last finishing touches into place:
some pillows from your bedroom down the hall;
a box of plastic jewellery
and some wooden food

Your children sit in a patient row under one of the
table legs:
the gangly-legged bear lies on his side staring blindly
back at the knowing silky one.
You feel warm and satisfied, a job well done.

And then you walk away in search of something else,
and forget about it all.
Silky one eases herself up and follows,
without a backward glance.

You are in bed now, the curtains closed against the
day,
warm and sleepy.
Silky one has positioned herself at the end just
beyond your toes, legs out straight
as she lies on her side with the warmth of the sun
on her belly.
She is looking forward to an hour of stasis and
perhaps
of sleep.
You curl up with knees to chest and feel the crisp
edge
of the sheet on your top lip.
And you are gone.

You both step into the woods of sleep and face each
grinning.
Silky one has stood up straight and has a face the
same as yours.
You hold each other's hands and run until your legs

are moving faster than your bodies.
And on the bed in the curtained off bedroom,
two little bodies jerk and twitch together.

'You are flying together'

You haven't noticed that the silky one's face is yours
and she hasn't noticed that her paws are hands
and she's wearing bunny slippers just like the ones
you lost.
You tumble over and fall a long way down
through air and wait
for the bump
at the bottom
which doesn't come because you are flying together

above a town

which looks just like a town in a book about Christmas

you looked at this morning in the den you built

and have forgotten about.

Flying is so easy you think,

lifting up and pushing forward.

The silky one is smiling and so are you,

both of you,

as you fly and as you sleep.

And then, you think that you must remember you can fly when you wake up.

So you do wake up.

Now,

You are the silky one.

The door's ajar as it was before you slept and the dust particles are still dancing

in the line of sunlight
that pierces the half gloom of the room.

Stretching all four legs as far as they will stretch
a shiver ecstatically follows itself down your back.
You picture the park.
You feel a need for the greenness
and the vastness and the twinkles of the park,
beyond
the house.
You want it now.
You're ready.
From down to up in a flash and on the floor with a
thump.
Both of you skipping out of the room and down the
hall
to find the little one's
mummy one,
to get things done.

Outside is still there.
Wind and roar and sun and sparkle.

The small one is quiet, looking at the leaves,
thinking about the wall;
the yellow slithery leaves of the weeping willow and how
she will walk along the wall
and jump off at the end;
perhaps fly off at the end.
You walk sensibly and purposefully,
hoping that your
four-legged momentum
will keep the party moving:
the wheels of the pram; the feet of the mummy one
and the desires of the little one,
just until the park is reached and the vast greenness can
be sniffed and seen,
felt and shared.

The small one's wails about the need
to be on the
wall
stop the movement.

Up, out and onto the wall,
bundled inside layers of warmth,
she watches her feet and feels the height of the wall.
Jump, walk, skip, skip, balance.

She's feeling it too –
that sense of being on the edge of more.
Fast across the green to the other side,
because you must.
The small one and the mummy one are shapes in
your peripheral vision;
you are a kite soaring across the grass in a one
dimensional picture
of happiness
and anxiety.

Sound and scent dance around you as you
dart and skip from place to place,
unable to tear yourself away because of the pull and the need.

You know the small one is running and falling and laughing,
wanting to catch you,
but you have to finish your search before you go to her.
Check the changes in the outside world;
leave your messages
for the others;
make it clear you will do anything for this small one.

Enough; you turn and run to the bundled up movement
on the grass,
struggling to right herself because of the quilted suit
and the plastic boots.

She looks at you with relief
as you stand and wait for her uprightness,
lick face, taste sweetness, continue.
Now.
Return to small one,
You.

You're on the field in your red, plastic boots
surrounded by whiteness with a silky one lick
licking your face.
Her silky brownness and kind, kind eyes;
her reassuring knowledge of you makes you feel
stable,
wrapped gently in a soft, soft blanket of certainty.
You open your eyes.

You have flown from the field and awoken in some
other bed,
Not curtained off but quiet.
Body changed.

The light through the curtain is blue and sharp and reminds you
of how much you used to like it under the blanket roof
of the dining table den,
with the pink light and the first silky one.

You stretch your legs and forget that you can't,
and utter a sound which brings a silkiness to your side.
Lick hand, taste sweetness, lick hand.
You turn on your side and look into the eyes of this silky one,
standing,
his calm brown eyes and his grey white head,
waiting for you.
You watch your hand as it touches the fur on the tip of his nose,
and as you stroke from grey full stop to soft,

soft top of head in a slow, gentle pat of gratitude.
And again.
And again.
So then,
when later, by the back door, you struggle
to bundle yourself into your thick waxed jacket,
and you have to lean against the wall and curse
under your breath
as you ease yourself into your green welly boots,

you will know that you owe
this silky one
(and all the other silky ones that came in between)
all that you have that makes sense.

That the warmth that you feel,
the lift in your step,
and the still gently glowing sense of purpose
somewhere beyond,

that takes you out into the greenness

and the wind,

is a silky shaped blessing
from the time before,
when you knew that you were at the heart of all
and on the edge of something else.

And the silky one, as he trots by your side,
alive to the moment,
the here and now,
will marvel at you
(as all the silky ones have done)
will marvel at your ability
to push aside the heaviness
and put one foot in front of the next
so very easily.

Identity Theft

Here's my lanyard. Take it. Do.
My identity tag; my member's badge.
Signalling to the rest of you – I'm safe –
I can be trusted. No stranger or interloper.
Plastic proof: I am meant to be here.

Have it. Put it in a drawer and forget about it.
Put it with old keys and lost glasses.
Or throw it away. Risk it. Perhaps
someone will rummage through the bin,
find my lanyard and use it to create a new
identity for themselves. I hope not.

That would be so sad.

No. Good luck to them. I hope they hang it
round their neck and find that fitting in
suits them. Me? I fancy being a stranger

for a while. A danger. Photo-less and free.

I'll wander corridors unchecked and delight in being me.

Made in the USA
Monee, IL
03 May 2026

49437972R00020